Mastering Bitcoin:

The Essential Guide to Bitcoin and Cryptocurrency Technologies, Mining, Investing and Trading

Tim Barnes

© Copyright 2017 by Tim Barnes

All rights reserved.

The follow eBook is reproduced below with the goal of providing information that is as accurate and reliable as possible. Regardless, purchasing this eBook can be seen as consent to the fact that both the publisher and the author of this book are in no way experts on the topics discussed within and that any recommendations or suggestions that are made herein are for entertainment purposes only. Professionals should be consulted as needed prior to undertaking any of the action endorsed herein.

This declaration is deemed fair and valid by both the American Bar Association and the Committee of Publishers Association and is legally binding throughout the United States.

Furthermore, the transmission, duplication or reproduction of any of the following work including specific information will be considered an illegal act irrespective of if it is done electronically or in print. This extends to creating a secondary or tertiary copy of the work or a recorded copy and is only allowed with express written consent from the Publisher. All additional right reserved.

The information in the following pages is broadly considered to be a truthful and accurate account of facts and as such any inattention, use or misuse of the information in question by the reader will render any resulting actions solely under their purview. There are no scenarios in which the publisher or the original author of this work can be in any fashion deemed liable for any hardship or damages that may befall them after undertaking information described herein.

Additionally, the information in the following pages is intended only for informational purposes and should thus be thought of as universal. As befitting its nature, it is presented without assurance regarding its prolonged validity or interim quality. Trademarks that are mentioned are done without written consent and can in no way be considered an endorsement from the trademark holder.

Table of Contents

Introduction 5

Chapter 1: Bitcoin and Cryptocurrency Technologies 7

Chapter 2: Bitcoin Mining 23

Chapter 3: Investing in Bitcoins 34

Chapter 4: Blockchain Technology 43

Chapter 5: How to Invest in Bitcoins 54

Chapter 6: Trading in Bitcoins 71

Conclusion 91

Introduction

Congratulations on downloading this book and thank you for doing so.

The following chapters will discuss everything that you need to know about Bitcoins. You will learn what Bitcoin is, how it is generated and how it is mined. In recent years, Bitcoin has become one of the world's most popular cryptocurrency.
It is a digital currency that is encrypted to keep it from being compromised.

In the last couple of years, Bitcoin has captured the attention of the world due to its phenomenal growth and its wide, expansive and global reach. Its value has risen from just $100 in 2012 to a maximum of $5000 in 2017. While it is very volatile in nature, many individuals and organizations continue to invest in it, and many are making attractive returns on a regular basis.

By reading this book, you will learn how to trade in Bitcoins and how to receive Bitcoins as a payment solution for your businesses. Since Bitcoin has gained such worldwide approval by so many businesses, offering it as a payment solution for your business is something you need to consider. Your customers will be pleased to have an added payment option, and it will likely bring in additional business.

The phenomenal growth of Bitcoin and the opportunity for investors to earn a residual income have attracted many people as well as organization, including fund managers and retirement schemes. You, too, can now learn how to invest in this digital currency, how to use it for business, how to buy, sell or spend it or even send to family and friends.

There are plenty of books on this subject on the market, so thanks again for choosing this one! Every effort was made to ensure it is full of as much useful information as possible, please enjoy!

Chapter 1: Bitcoin and Cryptocurrency Technologies

What is Bitcoin?

By definition, Bitcoin is a type of digital currency that was created online and is held electronically. Bitcoin is a good example of a type of money commonly referred to as cryptocurrency.

This type of digital currency is not printed like British Pounds or Canadian dollars.

Instead, they are produced by individuals and businesses around the world using special software programs that are capable of handling complex mathematical problems.

What Is a Cryptocurrency?

The term cryptocurrency refers to a digital media of exchange. This media uses shared transaction ledgers and cryptography to create a traceable, secure, stable and anonymous monetary system.

The name cryptocurrency is derived from the use of cryptography, a technique used to encrypt messages to ensure they are transmitted privately and securely.

Cryptography is also useful because it enables authentication and security of data. Plenty of the technology and secrecy used by cryptographers is used in cryptocurrencies, ensuring they are secure and trustworthy.

More about Bitcoin

Bitcoin was created in 2008 by a respected developer who goes by the pseudo-name Satoshi Nakamoto. It is not controlled by any Reserve bank or Central Bank but is a decentralized currency with increasing popularity.

Its circulation is managed and overseen by a group of users who ensure that all transactions are secured, fulfilled and recorded.

The backbone of Bitcoin is something known as Blockchain. The Blockchain is a ledger that is visible to the public and lets any interested person check and verify any Bitcoin transaction.

Transactions can be traced back all the way to the first one ever made through Blockchain.

With time, Bitcoin gained much-needed recognition by Internet users, business owners, and various online communities. After the 2013 Cyprus banking crisis, the value of Bitcoin more than doubled.

Many people thought their money was not very secure in banks and preferred to have it in digital form. Many of them converted their money to Bitcoins.

Shortly after that, the Chinese discovered the importance of Bitcoin and invested in it. Its value skyrocketed and has remained high since. The transaction fees charged when using Bitcoins are very low especially compared to credit card charges, bank fees, and PayPal charges.

Credit card companies and banks often want as much personal information about you as possible. However, Bitcoin respects your privacy and will not request such personal information from you. It is also very secure, and hackers cannot penetrate it because it would be too costly for them. On the contrary, credit cards are very prone to hacking and personal details are easily compromised.

Privacy When Using Bitcoin

One of the best features of Bitcoin is its privacy. It is a very private cryptocurrency that does not care who you are or where you are. Bitcoin and its Blockchain of records provide users with ultimate control over their money. There is no consent needed from banks, parents or governments. This is very different to what we are used to when it comes to banks and common currencies.

Bitcoin uses wallets similar to bank accounts. These are different because they can never be frozen by anyone. On the contrary, bank accounts can be frozen on the orders of a court of law, by the government or even the bank on its own volition.

The technological design of Bitcoins is such that it is decentralized and anyone can use it. As a user, you can shop online, use it to pay for goods and services, save it in a wallet and watch its value appreciate and so much more. Bitcoins can also be used offline.

Numerous businesses accept Bitcoins for payment. They include local restaurants, shops, grocery stores, fuel stations and many others. Even non-government, non-profit organizations such as Wikipedia accept Bitcoin donations. The use of Bitcoin is very legal and can be used in a variety of ways.

Bitcoin Is International

It is important to appreciate that Bitcoin is used across many countries and not just the US. It is used in countries such as Argentina, China, Chile, Brazil, France, Japan and many others. Anyone is free to use this cryptocurrency. Any interested person can receive or send it over the Internet to any destination around the world. Its use enables commerce, promotes business, facilitates payments and does not present any exchange rate problems or fees.

Bitcoin does not have any age restrictions, and anyone can use Bitcoin online. People interested in working for Bitcoin or using Bitcoins can receive help and advice online. For instance, websites such as CoinHR assist people needing jobs with Bitcoin. There are also social media websites such as Facebook that have groups that assist people who wish to do business using Bitcoins.

When working for Bitcoin, you may find yourself working for someone located halfway around the world. This is because Bitcoin is international and is used by people all around the world.

Getting Started with Bitcoin

It is a fact that Bitcoin is the world's leading and most popular digital currency. It continues to grow as more and more people across the globe continue to learn about its impressive potential.

There is not one individual or entity that owns Bitcoin. You may think of it like email. It is a form of technology that anyone can use, but not one single company owns it. Therefore, banks, organizations, and governments cannot stop anyone from using, sending or receiving Bitcoins. While this sounds like great news to most people, there is the danger that there is no place to seek recourse should things go wrong.

Where to Keep Your Bitcoins

Therefore, never let untrustworthy people handle your Bitcoins. Neither let them keep it for you or send it to them. Instead, you need to find a trustworthy place to keep your Bitcoins. For this, you will need a Bitcoin Wallet.

A Bitcoin Wallet is defined as an application program that enables you to receive and send Bitcoins. This digital wallet also allows you to keep track of your Bitcoin income and expenditure.

There is not just one single Bitcoin Wallet but many different ones. They have different features and also function differently so before you download one, it is good you learn how to choose a good Bitcoin wallet.

When it comes to Bitcoin wallets, it is very important that you know, and trust who is in charge of the private keys necessary for spending your Bitcoins. These private keys can be compared to banks that hold your money, so trust here is very important. However, most trustworthy, reputable Bitcoin Wallets often let their users be in charge of their private keys.

If you are the only one in the whole world in charge of your private keys, then no one else can access your Bitcoin Wallet, meaning it is very secure. But it also means that no one can assist you should you lose your password or other access to the wallet. This is why it is advisable to divide your Bitcoins into several different wallets, just in case.

Bitcoin Price

The price of Bitcoin is determined by supply and demand. However, the supply of Bitcoin is limited to 21 million bitcoins. This limitation coupled with ever increasing demand means the price goes up very fast.

While the price may fluctuate on a day-to-day basis, it will continue to increase as its usage worldwide increases. In 2011, the price of 1 Bitcoin was less than $1. Today, in 2017, 1 Bitcoin is more than $4,400.

If this trend continues, then in the not too distant future, one Bitcoin would be worth tens, if not hundreds, of dollars.

The Bitcoin Exchanges

If you want to buy Bitcoins, then the best way to do so is through a trusted exchange. Please note that the exchange rate varies at each Bitcoin Exchange. This is why some people will buy Bitcoins at one Exchange and then sell them at another.

If you find that one Bitcoin Exchange constantly has higher prices than others, then this could be a sign of trouble, and you should give it a wide berth. You should do your research and find out which are the best and most trusted Bitcoin Exchanges.

Also, avoid making any Exchange in your wallet. Instead, you should transfer any Bitcoins you buy to your personal wallet. You will then always be in control of your Bitcoins. There is a list of trusted Bitcoins available online so search for it and use one that is highly recommended.

Bitcoin Transactions

All Bitcoin transactions are usually visible worldwide and are recorded on the ledger known as Blockchain. Blockchain is Bitcoin's worldwide ledger that records all its transactions. These transactions are super fast, especially when compared to transactions via traditional payment platforms.

Once a Bitcoin transaction is visible on the Blockchain ledger, it generally becomes acceptable. Even then, it is possible that a transaction may not be visible on the network immediately.

While Bitcoin is relatively new when compared to other payment systems, its technology keeps getting better and better. In fact, many are of the opinion that a major bug is unlikely to hit the system. Therefore, more and more people are likely to start using this popular cryptocurrency.

Cryptocurrencies

A cryptocurrency is essentially a virtual or digital currency that makes use of cryptography technology to secure it. This makes it very difficult for anyone to counterfeit it or infiltrate the system and compromise it.

One of the most alluring features of a cryptocurrency is its organic nature. This basically means that a cryptocurrency is not issued by a government or regulated by a central bank. This makes it virtually immune to government manipulation and interference.

The anonymous nature of cryptocurrencies has many benefits to users. However, there are some disadvantages. For instance, they are well suited for use in various illegal activities such as tax evasion and money laundering.

One of the best-known cryptocurrencies in the world is Bitcoin. Bitcoin was launched in 2009 and was the first cryptocurrency to gain worldwide publicity. As of 2015, there were over 14 million bitcoins available all worth an estimated $3.4 billion. This makes it the leading cryptocurrency in the world, having overtaken others such as PPCoin, NameCoin, and LiteCoin.

What Are the Pros and Cons of Cryptocurrencies?

One of the benefits of a cryptocurrency is that it makes sending and receiving money between two individuals or organizations very easy, fast and convenient. Funds are transferred seamlessly through use of private and public keys specifically for the interest of security.

Transfer of funds from one account or user to another is done at very minimal fees as opposed to the steep charges often incurred when using formal financial institutions.

The cryptocurrency Bitcoin stores all activity on a ledger known as the Blockchain. All transactions that have ever been undertaken using Bitcoin are registered here. All these transactions are instantly visible to users all over the world.

Blockchain transactions have very limited exposure to hackers and can be viewed on any computer running the Bitcoin software.

One of the dangers of Bitcoin is that since there is no central repository, a computer crash can completely wipe out a digital cryptocurrency balance. Backing up such important data is absolutely essential just in case anything goes wrong.

Bitcoins fluctuate widely because the price or value is based on supply and demand. This can greatly affect the worth of an investment or a payment at the time of conversion.

It is also noteworthy that Bitcoin and other cryptocurrencies are not immune to hacking. Hackers have managed to penetrate its security system over 40 times and stolen large amounts of Bitcoins. Even then, many in the business and finance sectors are excited to have a currency with such value and reach that is outside the control of governments.

Cryptocurrency Technology

Some technologies can be defined as landmark developments in the history of advances in technology. The Internet of Money (IoM), also known as cryptocurrency has introduced new ways of transacting and trading.

The very first cryptocurrency was known as ecash system and was developed way back in 1983. Then in 2008 came a man named Satoshi Nakamoto, a brilliant mathematician. He came up with the Bitcoin concept in a research paper. In his paper, Satoshi introduces bitcoins as a virtual or digital currency that can work as an online currency.

Bitcoin is implemented as an open source code. It also happens to be the first decentralized virtual payment system in the world. This digital cryptocurrency essentially eliminated regulations and payment gateways.

Traditional payment systems such as PayPal, Visa, MasterCard and others make use of gateways that charge rather stiff fees and charges. They also increase the operation time significantly so that it takes longer to process payments compared to cryptocurrencies.

Cryptocurrencies eliminate this gateway and introduce peer-to-peer or P2P transactions. The P2P transactions eliminate the time wastage as well as the exorbitant fees and charges.

Bitcoin Transactions

Bitcoin does not operate via 16-bit encryptions, physical address or emails. Instead, Bitcoins operate on random QR codes each of which is 160 bits. Bitcoin system allows peer-to-peer transfer of currency without a gateway.

Each transaction uses what is known as a public-key cryptography to prevent hacking or interference and manipulation of the data. It is then verified separately using another code and the payee's private key.

Even then, any Bitcoin platform will demand genuine identities from users, such as an email id.

Bitcoin and cryptocurrency transfers are ultra transparent. As soon as a transaction is concluded, it immediately appears in the public domain which is instantly updated.

Then anyone who, so wishes can confirm that a certain transaction took place. This largely ensures transparency and safety guarantees are in place.

It is the transparency that guarantees the safety and security such that no user can challenge the transactions. This also makes it super-difficult for any hacker to try and penetrate the system to commit acts of fraud.

Satoshi, the creator of the program, was quoted stating that it is the first non-trust system being decentralized.

Cryptocurrencies have other benefits too. For instance, Reserve Banks and Central Banks spend large amounts of their resources in printing and transporting currencies and in the regulation of traditional currencies. This is not the case when it comes to Bitcoins. It does not cost a single cent to generate Bitcoins while miners are handsomely rewarded when they generate cryptocurrency.

Bitcoin Technology

By now you are aware that Bitcoin accounts are operated as random QR codes each of which is 160 bits. The fact that transactions are anonymous and not regulated by governments continues to worry some people around the world.

Reputable media organizations like Wall Street Journal, New York Time and the Guardian have engaged their readers about these concerns. However, according to the lead developer at

Bitcoin, the anonymity issues, while greater than those of other online transactions, are less than those presented by cash payments. Facts indicate that other forms of payment gateways are riskier and more vulnerable to hacking and fraud. For instance, credit cards can be compromised where unauthorized persons gain access to personal information which they use fraudulently.

Chapter 2: Bitcoin Mining

What is Bitcoin Mining?

The term Bitcoin mining refers to the process by which any Bitcoin transactions are conducted, verified and then added to a public ledger. This ledger, which is known as the Blockchain, is publicly available to all Bitcoin users so any Bitcoin transaction can be checked, confirmed and verified.

In fact, any person with a connected device and has the necessary software can easily engage in Bitcoin mining. The mining process itself is designed to be challenging as well as resource intensive so that the number of blocks miners can find each day is regular.

Blocks are defined as Bitcoin files or just files that contain data about the Bitcoin network is stored. Therefore, data about a transaction is stored in a block. The entire chain of blocks is referred to as the Blockchain.

A block records either some or all of the data about a Bitcoin transaction. This data will usually not have been entered into any other blocks. Blocks, therefore, act like records or ledgers where entries are made.

Bitcoin Mining Process

Bitcoin mining is a process that involves the compilation of the most recent transactions into ledgers referred to as blocks. The process also involves completion of a challenging computer puzzle.

Whoever completes this puzzle first gets their transaction registered in the Blockchain. There is a reward for the one who can complete the mining process first. The reward includes the transaction fees and any newly released Bitcoins.

Block Reward

When a block is mined, it generates new Bitcoins which are then released. The block reward refers to the amount or quantity of new Bitcoins released. For every 210,000 blocks that are released, the block reward is divided into 2. This happens on average every 4 years.

For instance, the block reward began in 2009 at 50 Bitcoins and was 25 Bitcoins in 2014. This figure will continue to decrease and with the decrease comes more Bitcoins. Eventually, the total amount of Bitcoins will be released.

Bitcoin Mining Puzzles

Mining Bitcoins comes with puzzles that need to be solved. Sometimes the puzzles are difficult to solve, but sometimes they are simple. It all depends on the amount of effort being put in Bitcoin mining across the entire network.

The difficulty range is adjustable and paces itself purposely to keep the block discovery rate at a constant. Therefore, when increased computation power is needed, then the difficulty level will increase while lesser computational power means a lower difficulty level.

Bitcoin Mining Hardware

In the early days, Bitcoin miners used the CPU on regular desktop computers. Later on, users moved to the GPU or graphics processing units. These were considered more efficient when compared to CPUs.

Today, however, there is a piece of hardware known as ASIC that was specifically built to process Bitcoin mining. ASIC stands for Application-Specific Integrated Circuit. These have been used since 2013, and the latest ones are a much-improved version of the initial ones.

Today, Bitcoin mining has become very efficient with better computer designs regularly released in the market. When the mining process is done efficiently using a modern ASIC, then the process becomes profitable.

However, when using older ASIC models or GPUs and CPUs, then more energy is used, and the process will not be efficient.

Bitcoins are mined into existence. The process of Bitcoin mining serves two purposes. One of these is to release new Bitcoins while the other is to produce entries or transactions to the Blockchain.

The mining process involves compiling most recent Bitcoin transactions and solving a complex puzzle.

The rewards associated with Bitcoin mining are enough of an incentive. These rewards include transaction fees that are paid to the miner in the form of Bitcoins and newly released Bitcoins.

Who Can Mine Bitcoins?

The mining of Bitcoins has been decentralized. Now, just about any interested person can mine Bitcoins. All that is need is access to the internet through a device such as a PC and the right hardware.

Decentralization is the mainstay of Bitcoins security. The Bitcoin network normally decides on important decisions through consensus. Should any disagreements arise regarding blocks inclusion in the Blockchain, then a simple majority rule wins the day.

The 51% Attack

Sometimes organizations and individuals get a chance to control more than 50% of the mining power within Bitcoin's network. When this happens, then the organization or individual can corrupt the Blockchain. Such a situation is referred to as the 51% attack.

Such an attack could be devastating. The extent of its devastation would depend on the amount of mining power the Bitcoin network has. This means the security of the Bitcoin network largely depends on the amount of mining power that is employed.

You also need to know the size of the mining power used in a network. Part of the reward of Block mining is the block reward, and it refers to the new Bitcoins that are released and made available. Today, the block rewards provide the largest incentives for Bitcoin miners.

Transaction Fees

Since the block keeps diminishing with time, miners lose most of the incentive that they often rely on. This is the block reward. Now, with its diminishing prospect comes a security challenge for Bitcoin. This incentive could easily be replaced with transaction fees.

Miners may get to receive a transaction fee which is simply a tiny amount of the Bitcoins they mine. This tiny amount is calculated and awarded to the miner who mined the Bitcoins.

Currently, transaction fees are voluntary on the part of a sender. Therefore, users may decide to pay miners a transactional fee as an incentive.

Challenges in Bitcoin Mining

The difficulty or challenges that Bitcoin miners experience often depend on a couple of factors. These include the amount of effort being put in Bitcoin mining across the network.

There is a protocol provided on how to go about the mining process. If correctly followed, then the network will automatically adjust itself to accommodate the new Bitcoins.

The aim of the adjustment is essential to maintain a constant rate of block discovery. The network adjusts the difficulty level of mining Bitcoins every two weeks or after every 2016 blocks.

It is important to note that when there is more computational power adopted, the difficulty level increases, while less computer power results in reduced difficulty levels. The difficulty level is therefore adjusted to make mining easier.

Basically, when more people are mining, then the difficulty level goes up while it goes down when there are fewer people mining Bitcoins.

The total payout to miners will depend on transaction fees, the current Bitcoin price, and the block reward. Even then, each miner will receive a payout depending on the total number of miners out there because they all have to share the spoils.

What Is the Hardware Used in Bitcoin Mining?

If you want to mine Bitcoins, then all you need is the appropriate hardware and a connected device. While initial hardware used included CPUs and GPUs, today, there are advanced ASICS that are used by miners.

When older ASICS models or CPUs and GPUs are used for Bitcoin mining, then the cost of energy becomes higher than the amount of revenue generated.

To be efficient when mining Bitcoins, it is important to ensure that only the latest ASICS version is used. But with this latest hardware, the difficulty level has risen exponentially.

Today's miners feel greatly incentivized due to the high Bitcoin prices as well as speculative nature of this cryptocurrency.

Miners also get to enjoy some form of power, especially when it comes to decision making.

People who have control of mining power also have a say regarding protocol changes and so on.

Common Bitcoin mining tools are produced by companies such as Butterfly Labs, Hash Fast, Bitfury and so on. Customers can purchase or lease the equipment they need for Bitcoin mining.

What Are Bitcoin Mining Pools?

When mining Bitcoins, miners have to solve a puzzle. Now the miner who comes up with the solution first receives a reward. The chance that a miner will be the one to first find a solution to the puzzle depends on the number of miners in the entire Bitcoin network. Therefore, the more the mining power, the better.

Miners with a tiny percentage of this mining power will have very little chance of earning the mining rewards. As a miner, you need to purchase a card for an amount, usually thousands of dollars. Yet such a card only awards you about 0.001% of the mining power in the entire network.

This percentage is too low to enable you to find the next block by solving the puzzle. From here, it gets even tougher because most likely another miner will soon find the solution. As a miner, you may probably not even be able to recover your costs and initial investment. This is where mining pools come in handy.

Electricity Costs Affiliated with Bitcoin Mining

People who mine Bitcoins receive a reward for their efforts. Miners who manage to solve a Bitcoin mining puzzle first receive a reward. Those with very little mining power have a very limited chance of solving the next puzzle and releasing the next block on their own.

One of the major costs that miners incur is that of electricity and hardware purchase. Electricity is required for ventilation and cooling and also for powering the Bitcoin mining equipment.

Most miners try to locate their operations close to areas or regions with affordable electricity. In the US, one of the largest mining operations is found in Washington State, close to the Columbia River.

Here, there is an abundance of very cheap, hydroelectric power. The firm running this operation is MegaBigPower. There are servers in Iceland belonging to CloudHashing, a Bitcoin mining company operating in that country. The climate in Iceland and other Nordic countries is very cold most of the year.

Regulating Bitcoin Operations

A while ago, the US Internal Revenue Service provided some taxation guidelines for cryptocurrencies such as Bitcoin. The guidelines provide that the income generated from Bitcoin mining operations can be considered as income from self-employment. As such, the IRS reasons that it should be subjected to tax.

But according to a government financial crimes enforcement network, Bitcoin miners are not considered to be Money Transmitters under the relevant US laws and should therefore not be subjected to taxation under these laws.

To cap matters on Bitcoin mining, we have demonstrated that this is a process through which new Bitcoins enter into circulation. The total number of Bitcoins approved for circulation is 21 million BTC.

As more and more computer power is used to generate Bitcoins, the complexity of the puzzles increases to maintain an acceptable increase in Bitcoin numbers and to ensure the profitability of miners is in check.

Chapter 3: Investing in Bitcoins

In 2017, the price of Bitcoin hit the $4600 mark. The price keeps fluctuating, but analysts expect it to head towards the $5000 mark before the end of the year. Plenty of investors have put some of their money in this cryptocurrency. Some venture capitalists have invested their funds there in the hundreds of millions.

Compare this to 2012 when Bitcoin firms were only able to raise just over $2 million. This virtual currency has experienced phenomenal growth regarding merchants and users despite price fluctuations. Many people, institutions, funds, and organizations are investing in Bitcoin and reaping the rewards.

How to Invest in Bitcoins

With the price of Bitcoin soaring over the years, amateur investors have been jumping into this market with the hope of cashing in. However, cautious financial advisers are skeptical about this currency and are worried the surge might lead to a bubble burst.

For a regular person, the best way to invest in Bitcoins is simply to go out and buy some. The purchase process is a pretty simple and straightforward process. There are quite some firms that deal in buying and selling of Bitcoins.

These are found both in the USA and all around the globe. US investors should opt to deal with Coinbase, one of the most reputable Bitcoin companies.

Coinbase sells Bitcoins to investors at a rate of 1% above the prevailing market rates. This firm can link investor's bank accounts with their Coinbase wallets. With this connection, customers will easily transfer funds from one account to another.

If you sign up at Coinbase, you will be able to log into your account and then purchase Bitcoins whenever you wish. You could also set up your account such that you purchase Bitcoins on a regular basis.

For instance, you could set it up to purchase Bitcoins worth $100 every 1st day of the month. This will require you to set up an auto-buy with Coinbase. However, you should be careful when setting up this kind of arrangement.

Automatic purchases will not help you keep track of Bitcoin prices so you may sometimes purchase very expensively only for the prices to fall shortly after that.

Also, remember that Coinbase is definitely not a Bitcoin exchange which means you will not buy Bitcoins directly but through a Third Party which means you get to pay more for your Bitcoins. This also means you have to wait a little longer for the transactions to go through.

If you are interested in buying Bitcoins at a regular exchange in America, then the best choice is BitStamp. Bitstamp allows you to trade directly with other people, usually buyers and sellers.

This way, you get to purchase Bitcoins directly from sellers. It is advisable to use this route to avoid the middleman. The middleman always charges a fee for their service, and this makes your trades expensive.

At BitStamp, you get to pay a small fee which starts at 0.5%. Traders and anyone else who has spent over $150,000 on the site can pay fees as low as 0.2%. An even better way of investing in Bitcoin is via what is called Local Bitcoins. This is one of the most popular ways of investing in BTC offline.

Local Bitcoins will link you up with sellers. The site links up buyers with sellers and allows them to trade at rates they agree upon. Normally, Bitcoins will be locked in escrow, a popular payment system that makes online deals and trades more credible.

Now, when purchasing or investing in BTC, the Bitcoins will be locked in an escrow account and released by the seller once they receive payment for the BTC. Should a dispute arise, then a case can be filed where both the buyer and seller can tell their side of the story.

It is very important that you take all the necessary precautions when trading in Bitcoins offline. For instance, meeting in a public place and bringing a trusted friend or close family member along. It is better to be cautious than sorry.

The bottom line is, according to venture capitalists, Bitcoins are here to stay. Many people have invested in Bitcoins and are enjoying very attractive returns. For instance, if you invested $1000 in Bitcoins in 2010, you would be worth $20 million today.

How to Buy Bitcoins

Buying Bitcoins is a simple and easy process if you know how to. Surprisingly, not many people know how to. However, it is important to understand the entire process of how to buy BTC.

Sign up for a Bitcoin wallet

The first step in buying Bitcoins is getting a Bitcoin wallet. This is a digital wallet where your Bitcoins will be kept. A Bitcoin wallet is like an app or account which you need to open. Websites such as www.blockchain.info can guide you on how to download the BTC wallet.

The process will involve filling out an online form where you provide minimal details such as an email address and so on. This is a process that should take you not more than one or two minutes. The account itself would look largely similar to online banking accounts that most banks use.

As soon as you have your Bitcoin wallet available, then you are ready to start receiving Bitcoins. You can use regular currency such as dollars or pounds to purchase your first Bitcoins. All you need to do is visit a Bitcoin exchange site. There are a good number of these, and one of them is Coinbase.

Bitcoin Exchange

Bitcoin exchanges accept payment through traditional payment platforms. Therefore, you can access your funds on your credit card, bank account or any other to pay for Bitcoins at the exchange. Once you buy the Bitcoins, the Bitcoins will be transferred to your wallet.

The Bitcoin exchange and your Bitcoin wallet do not have to be from the same organization. You are at liberty as to which organization you get your wallet from and where you purchase your Bitcoins. The most important factor is that you select reputable institutions that are trustworthy and reliable.

Just to point out, a Bitcoin exchange is similar in operation to a forex exchange bureau. This means it is a place where you can take your currency, such as dollars, and exchange these for Bitcoins. For instance, exchange USD for BTC. It is just that the BTC cannot be transferred to your bank account or other formal payment platforms. And hence the reason you need a Bitcoin wallet.

Caution

As a precaution, ensure that your Bitcoin wallet is very secure and safe. Therefore, avoid, where you can, from getting a Bitcoin wallet from the exchange you will use. Exchanges offer Bitcoin exchange services, and their wallets may not be the most secure.

They often advise their clients not to keep their Bitcoins in very large amounts or for long periods of time in their wallets. Always search for a Bitcoin wallet offering a multi-signature provision.

Bitcoin Wallet and Your Private Key

The general belief among members of the public is that a Bitcoin Wallet is for storing Bitcoins. This might be true in some sense, but technically, it is not. Actually, Bitcoins are stored as public and private keys. These keys consist of a lengthy string of letters and numbers. These numbers are then linked together via an encryption algorithm.

You can compare these keys to actual security features in regular payment portals. For instance, the public key is similar in various ways to IBAN, or bank account number.

It serves mainly as the address shown to the public. Similarly, the private keys can compare well to an ATM pin. It is used mostly to guard your Bitcoin wallet and to only permit Bitcoin transactions. Therefore, in your Bitcoin wallet, all that is stored there is your private key.

Your Bitcoin wallet should be stored as securely as possible to prevent any fraudulent and unauthorized activity. One very important safeguard is to encrypt your wallet with a very strong password. You should also consider a cold storage strategy such as storing the wallet offline.

This is a great way of keeping it safe and secure. Firms such as Coinbase use a very secure multi-signature facility, referred to as MultiSig Vault. If you open a Bitcoin wallet with them, then you should sign up for this vault to secure your keys.

Using Your Bitcoins

Once you purchase your Bitcoins and secure them in your Bitcoin wallet, you are then free to spend them in any way that you please. You may, for instance, purchase goods, send to a friend or even pay for services.

Sending Bitcoins

Sending Bitcoins is pretty easy. You will not send actual Bitcoins to your receiver. You will simply need your private key as well as the address of the recipient. Therefore, you will need your recipient's address to send them Bitcoins or even to make a payment. If you sell your Bitcoins at the exchange, then you will receive its equivalent value in local currency. This amount can then be transferred to your bank account.

Bitcoin Exchange Rate

The price of Bitcoin varies from country to country even though Bitcoin is homogenous all around the world. The reason for this is arbitrage. Arbitrage is the process where a person buys something so they can sell it instantly at a profit.

While demand and supply do play a big role in determining the price or value of Bitcoin in countries around the world, arbitrage also plays a huge role. For instance, Bitcoin attracts a premium of 20 - 25% in India and about 40% in South Korea.

There are many places where Bitcoin is accepted as a form of payment. These include grocery stores, department stores, online retail outlets and others. The list keeps increasing each month with more and more businesses accepting Bitcoins. This is causing Bitcoin to gain not just local but global acceptance as well. Some countries like Japan have accepted and endorsed the use of Bitcoins as a formal mode of payment for goods and services.

Chapter 4: Blockchain Technology

Blockchain Definition

The term Blockchain has already been defined. In short, it is a public ledger of all Bitcoin transactions that have already taken place. Blockchain is constantly growing because transactions take place all the time. Each transaction has to have a public entry which is made on the Blockchain.

The Bitcoin Blockchain is definitely an ingenious invention. It was invented by a gentleman by the name Satoshi Nakamoto. Since its invention, it has grown and evolved into a truly impressive digital ledger.

Blockchain lets users distribute but not copy digital information. This very technology has provided the backbone for a new kind of Internet. While it has largely been used for Bitcoin transactions, it is now finding useful applications in other fields.

Blockchain as a distributed database

You can think of Blockchain as a single spreadsheet that is duplicated numerous times across vast computer networks distributed around the world. The spreadsheet on this network regularly and accurately updates the data in there. This is basically what Blockchain technology is all about.

While Blockchain was largely designed for use with Bitcoins, it is now finding applications in many different fields, especially the financial sector. Institutions in this sector such as banks are adopting the use of Blockchain technology to keep their own incorruptible records of transactions.

Blockchain data is never held at a central area. This means the information held there is readily accessible and verifiable and completely public. Hackers are therefore not able to penetrate the technology to corrupt the data or use the information in an unauthorized manner.

Blockchain as Google Docs

Now think about sharing an MS Word document with a friend. You ask them to make changes but cannot see the changes until your friend sends the documents back to you. This means you cannot see the changes until you eventually receive the revised MS Word document. Modern databases work like this.

However, with Google docs, both parties can access a document and make changes at the same time, with the other party viewing the changes in real time. This is similar to Blockchain technology. The technology allows users to view and access records simultaneously. This kind of technology is useful not just with Bitcoins but in many other industries. Think about legal documents, banking, finance and mortgage world, sales and so many others.

Blockchain is robust and durable

Blockchain technology can again be compared to a robust Internet. This is because it stores blocks of information across the entire network. This way, no one controls it, and there is no possibility of failure at any single point.

Since the creation of Bitcoin back in 2008, it has operated on Blockchain and has not faced any significant disruptions. Any challenges that Bitcoin has experienced are limited to mismanagement and hacking. Similarly, the Internet has been around for about 30 years and has proven to be quite durable with an excellent track record. Blockchain follows closely in its footsteps.

Blockchain is incorruptible and transparent

Some of the most interesting aspects of Blockchain include the transparency and incorruptible nature of the technology. The system checks for updates and refreshes the data automatically every 10 minutes. There is a reconciliation of all transactions which are known as blocks. From this we can note the following;

Blockchain is transparent. Data is added to the entire network and made public. This happens approximately every 10 minutes

Blockchain cannot be corrupted. Anyone attempting to alter data on the network will require large amounts of computing power which is virtually impossible to get.

Blockchain is a network of nodes

A node is simply a computer that is connected to a network via a client that validates and relays transactions. Blockchain uses such nodes where a client validates transactions and relays them across the network. A copy of the transactions is then sent to the node.

On the Blockchain, each and every node performs the functions of a network administrator. As the network is decentralized, each node joins voluntarily and has an incentive to join the network. This incentive, of course, is the chance to receive Bitcoins.

When Bitcoin was conceived, Blockchain was developed specifically to accommodate it. However, many now think Bitcoin is just one of many applications that can make use of Blockchain.

Decentralization of Blockchain

Within the Blockchain network, anything that occurs is basically a function of the entire network. This concept creates many possibilities such as managing transactions at the stock exchange. From this, we can conclude that Bitcoin is not controlled from one central place but rather from a network of interconnected computers.

Use of Blockchain Technology

Like many other forms of technology, users do not necessarily have to understand how exactly it functions. The strongest use of this technology is in the financial services sector. Plenty of major players in the sector have expressed their interest already. Its use could revolutionize the way financial transactions and services are handled.

Currently, users get a Bitcoin wallet which they use for their transactions. However, according to analysts, there will be plenty of exciting apps in the future that will help transform the way Bitcoin is used and help in identification process.

They will very likely include identity management for Bitcoin and for other Blockchain users. This way, online reputation, and identity will be decentralized.

Enhanced security with Blockchain

When data is stored at a central location, it is prone to many dangers such as hacking, theft, illegal use and so on. But when data is decentralized and stored all across the network, then it becomes difficult to access it. Computer hackers love centralized systems which always have vulnerable points.

Most common systems currently require a username and password to allow access to centralized information. However, with Blockchain, the information is encrypted so that compromising it is virtually impossible.

Blockchain is a second level network

In 2016 alone, Bitcoin users carried out transactions worth over $200,000 each day. This is because the network allows users to interact and transact directly with each other. Such level of security has prompted other businesses to seek to adopt this format for their operations.

Take for instance financial institutions such as Goldman Sachs. This firm believes that adopting a decentralized network such as Blockchain will enable them to speed up clearing and settlements and can, in the long run, help save financial institutions up to $6 billion annually.

In this scenario, the Internet is decentralized and has been quite stable for the past 25 years. It is considered a first-level network. Then we have Blockchain network which is also decentralized. It is the second-level network or a network within a network.

Blockchain possibly a new Web 3.0

With more attention being paid to Blockchain and its possibilities, many now consider it the new Web 3.0. Basically, Blockchain provides web users the opportunity to authenticate digital data and create value. This has many different applications today.

Crowdfunding

There are lots of exciting crowdfunding applications out there, such as GoFundMe. They are doing an excellent job by achieving their intended purposes even as they provide users with a direct say in how their affairs are managed. Blockchain can ensure that users are directly involved.

One crowdfunding application, based on Ethereum, which is decentralized, was able to raise an impressive $200 million in less than 2 months. Users were able to purchase tokens and participate in a vote on certain contracts. Unfortunately, this application was hacked because it wasn't very well planned.

Smart contracts

Ledgers such as those used on Blockchain enable development of simple contracts that come into play under specified conditions. Ethereum is an example of Blockchain technology that is still under development but is very promising.

Blockchain and Governance

Blockchain also finds a useful application in governance. Its use ensures openness and provides access to information by members of the public. Smart contracts on platforms ensure that results are open and transparent in events such as elections.

Blockchain and supply chain management

Many consumers around the world want to know that claims made by firms are actually true. With an open network and distributed network, this becomes something very easy to achieve.

Blockchain technology will ensure there is transparency in the operations of corporations, whether large or small and that customers can access the information they need in real time.

Transparency is important to consumers, and it comes with Blockchain-based time stamping that includes a location and a date. There are already firms that provide such services to their customers.

Blockchain and identity management

There is a need for better identification systems on the Internet. Many operations, including financial transactions, are hinged on the ability to verify the identity of a user.

The currently available remedies to counter security risks on the web are hardly reliable. Distributed ledgers such as Blockchain technology offer reliable solutions that can be adopted by governments, institutions, and organizations. Currently, there are tech companies working to develop SSL standard for Blockchain. This product is expected to be launched later in the year.

Blockchain and land title registration

Land titles are public documents that should be readily available to the public. Unfortunately, the documents and the records are very susceptible to fraud, and their administration is quite labor intensive.
Use of ledgers such as those on Blockchain can help provide a lasting solution to this challenge.

Today, a number of governments are implementing Blockchain solutions to addressing these challenges.

Use of such a secure system that is open to the public and is harder to corrupt is definitely a welcome development. It will enhance the security and credibility of public systems.

Blockchain and stock trading

Blockchains come in very handy in stock market trading especially when it comes to sharing settlement. Trade confirmations can be made almost instant if peer-to-peer computing technology is adopted.

Currently, tens of stock exchanges around the world are using prototypes of Blockchain designed specifically to handle trades and provide instant reports. It also means that others in the management chain such as custodians and clearing houses are removed from the chain.

Stock exchanges such as the ones in Australia, Japan, and Germany are trying out Blockchain prototypes. If successful, these will no doubt be imitated by other securities exchanges all around the world.

Chapter 5: How to Invest in Bitcoins

Bitcoin has been around since 2009, but it wasn't until 2013 that it started to attract attention from the financial sector. In that time, it had gained over 300% in value, and between 2012 and 2015 it gained over 400% in value. As of 2017, the value of the Bitcoin hit the $5000 mark.

Today, venture capitalists and investors from around the world continue to invest in this cryptocurrency. However, many investors still have questions that need to be answered. For instance, people want to know;

- How to prudently and properly invest in Bitcoins

- What important information they need to know

- How not to lose money

- How to add Bitcoin to their investment portfolio

- If investment in Bitcoin is still profitable

There is plenty of money to be made through a network such as Blockchain. And Bitcoin uses this technology. For over 20 years, people have profited from networks and the best one to invest in now is the Bitcoin cryptocurrency.

Therefore, if an investor puts their money on a network that is steadily growing, their investment is bound to grow exponentially. For instance, consider the incredible, exponential growth of users and investors in Bitcoin over the years;

2010 – There were 10,000 Bitcoin users

2012 – There were 100,000 Bitcoin users

2014 – The number grew to 1 million Bitcoin users and investors

2016 – Over 10 million Bitcoin users in the US and around the world

Bitcoin investment is different

Investing in Bitcoins is significantly different to investing in other securities or currencies. This applies to anyone who invests either directly by buying Bitcoins or through an exchange. Bitcoins varies in 2 different ways from other types of investments.

The volatility of Bitcoin

Bitcoin is a very volatile digital currency. In its lifetime, only 21 million Bitcoins will ever get into circulation. Each Bitcoin is further subdivided into hundred million decimals. This implies that any major incident such as an announcement can have a huge effect on this virtual currency.

Anyone considering the use of Bitcoin as a form of payment or optional currency will have to contend with its volatile nature. Investors are generally concerned that the currency may lose a good portion of its value by the time a transaction is processed.

Attraction to the securities market

At the securities market, traders are attracted to Bitcoin because of its steady and phenomenal growth. Traders are used to volatility and have the tools necessary to overcome it. While all other commodities were on a downward trend, only Bitcoin showed steady growth over the years. This cryptocurrency has caught the attention of investors in a big way.

Is Bitcoin a commodity or currency?

It is important to understand the nature of security before investing in it. Most consumers consider Bitcoin to be a form of digital currency that offers an alternative to hard currencies such as the dollar or the euro.

Bitcoin has characteristics that are very different to other currencies. It is not a coincidence that it rose to prominence at a time when forex and securities markets were not doing well. In its major scope, Bitcoin is basically a currency and a form of payment solution.

On the markets, however, Bitcoin lies in between commodities and currencies. Traders who accept Bitcoins as a form of payment actually increase its liquidity and also legitimacy.

Bitcoin investment is different to forex pairs

Plenty of traders and investors may already know about trading in foreign currencies. This has been a popular investment method adopted around the world. Investing in Bitcoins is different from forex trading.

The success of Bitcoin is not pegged on the performance of an economy or actions of a central bank. The only worry to Bitcoin from Central Banks is the threat of regulation. Bitcoin is also only valuable as a means of payment and nothing else.

Why people choose to invest in Bitcoin

- There are no taxes levied
- Account opening is absolutely free
- Transaction fees are very low and affordable
- All transactions are visible and transparent; the status of the account is always known
- No one can block your account
- No one will request for your personal information
- Transactions can never be reversed
- A complete history of transactions is always available
- Privacy and anonymity of account holders is enhanced

This list of benefits is not exhaustive and can go on and on. It is possible, just at a glance, to see the numerous benefits of investing in Bitcoins. But as a choice compared to other forms of investments, Bitcoin also stands out. Here is how;

- Bitcoin is immune to inflation and is not affected by regular parameters that cause inflation

- It shields investors from multiple fees, charges, and taxes

- It offers an alternative and is relatively secure albeit its volatility

Before investing, become technically competent

If you want to invest in Bitcoin, then it is important you learn a little bit more about cryptocurrencies. You also should be more informed about computers, technology and how they work.

It does not have to be comprehensive learning, just the basics will do. Such knowledge is crucial and will come in handy. Basic computer literacy and understanding things like cryptocurrency and Blockchain will enable you to make informed decisions and credible choices.

Some of the things you need to learn regarding technology include

- Backup your information

- Use credible and reliable anti-virus software and update it regularly

- Get a strong password that is long enough and uses letters, numbers and non-alphabetic characters

- Have different passwords for different online applications. Having just one password for all your online services is not a good idea

- Learn about data synchronization and why it is important

Have a well-defined investment strategy

Before investing in Bitcoins, you need to realize that nothing is for free and that there are some risks involved. Therefore, always consider investing only money that you can afford to lose.

You should make a determination about how much you would be willing to invest. Generally, if you have a financial asset, then you can consider investing about 1% - 10% of its value. If you are computer literacy is high, then you can consider investing up to 30% or even 50%. That is if you know what you are doing and can afford to take measured risks.

Financial assets include stocks, shares, bonds, and currencies. If they are worth more than $100,000, then you are lucky. You can consider investing anywhere between 1% and 10%.

However, if your financial assets are worth less than $100,000 then consider investing between 1% and 3% of that amount. This will help cushion you against any eventualities. You will still be able to grow your investment over time.

If your investment portfolio is less than $10,000, then you are still ahead. If you have a steady source of income, from employment or business, then you can consider investing about 5% of the amount into Bitcoins.

This rate can then increase all the way to 40%. If you have a retirement strategy or a saving and investment plan, then you can put aside 5% of your funds in Bitcoin. The outcome will impress you in one or two years' time.

Younger investors are at a much greater advantage. By investing their resources in Bitcoin now, they stand a chance to generate wealth and become financially stable in their twenties.

Purchase your first Bitcoins

To benefit from the Bitcoin boom, you have to purchase some Bitcoins first. Remember that 1 Bitcoin is subdivided into fractions of even 100,000 units so you can purchase as little or as much as you can afford.

To purchase Bitcoins, you will need a Bitcoin Wallet. However, how do you identify the best wallet? The best option is to go for a wallet that stores your keys offline.

Your Bitcoins will be in the form of keys. These keys should be stored offline on devices such as

- A USB drive or other mass media storage device
- An offline Bitcoin hardware wallet
- Or physical Bitcoins

If you can, you should avoid the following wallets

- Online web wallets such as Coinbase.com because these generally store keys on their servers

- Computer or mobile phone apps that require connectivity to the Internet

- Such wallets can be used for storing small amounts of Bitcoins, but once you start increasing your Bitcoins, then it is better to store them offline and keep them secure.

Here is the procedure for getting a secure wallet for your Bitcoins

Create a flash drive that is bootable. Ensure that you use permanently encrypted storage on this flash drive. You can then set up two distinct passwords. One of these will be to allow you to log into the drive and the other will be for encryption purposes.

Now create a cold wallet. This is essentially a wallet that is not connected to the Internet. You can do this using Electrum. Electrum is a type of Bitcoin wallet. Also, use Tails to load.

Now you need to come up with a complex password. Think about an alpha-numeric password that also consists of special characters such as the dollar or pound sign. Ensure that it is at least 20 characters long.

Write this password down on paper using a pen. With this complex password, you will easily be able to log into your wallet from any computer anywhere in the world and then access your Bitcoins.

In your Bitcoin wallet, ensure to check the option that allows you to view your transactions before signing in. The information will then be shared on the Blockchain.

Ensure that you come up with a Watch Only account. This can be created on the mobile phone or on the operating system of the computer. It is easy to do so with Electrum and Tails. This will enable you to view all your Bitcoin transactions but without being able to transact.

If you are to spend your Bitcoins or transact in them in any other way, then do ensure that you do so securely. You can use Tails rather than the Internet. Now make the transaction. Ensure that you view any transaction before signing. This transaction should then be saved onto a flash drive or other mass storage device offline.

Now once ready, upload the transaction to the Watch Only account. Remember that this account allows you to view your activity only, without transacting. This is to ensure your Bitcoins are safe and secure at all times. From this account, you can then upload the transaction to the Blockchain.

This way, you will be able to transact safely and securely and will ensure that your investment is safe from hackers. This same logic applies not just for Bitcoin but for other cryptocurrencies as well. It is very important to be safe at all times when transacting.

Some unique advantages of offline wallets

These wallets store private keys with secure areas of microcontrollers. These areas are protected so the keys cannot be transferred in a plain format

The wallets can be used interactively and securely without compromising the data held. They are completely protected from viruses, malware and other harmful software that may seek to steal information or compromise their security

Most of these wallets accept different types of cryptocurrencies and can hold them securely

Buying Bitcoins

One of the best places on the Internet to purchase Bitcoins is the website www.localbitcoins.com. It is a reputable, worldwide bazaar where anyone can purchase Bitcoins in almost any currency.

Most vendors here are very reputable, so chances of losing your investment are slim to none. Many of the traders here have been around for a long time and have made their names over this time so they can be considered trustworthy.

You will need to sign up with this Bitcoins vendor site; so, choose the security tab and then proceed to generate a pretty strong and secure password. Now find the drop-down menu and select seller. Do not just pick any seller. Here, you want to identify a seller who has large transaction volumes, completes trades very fast and very good ratings.

Each vendor has their own terms so go through the terms and ensure that you can comply if you like what you are presented with. If you agree to the terms, then you may agree and proceed.

After this stage is complete, you will proceed to indicate the number of Bitcoins you want to purchase. You may also leave a note for the vendor and probably seek their advice or comment on any concern you may have.

Most vendors are very helpful and will be happy to assist and advise you accordingly. There is often a button for you to click once you are ready to buy Bitcoins. Basically, you will be required to send some money using one or more of the specified methods. These could include the use of credit cards or debit cards, bank transfer or even digital platforms such as PayPal.

As soon you conclude the payment, let the system know that you have by clicking the relevant button. It only takes one minute or one hour before the transaction is processed and the Bitcoins you purchased awarded to you.

If the transaction proceeds as required and without any hitches or problems, then feel free to leave a positive feedback. The vendor will love it, and they will probably leave one for you too. After all, you will probably be back.

Transfer Bitcoins to offline wallet

Once the Bitcoins are credited to your www.localbitcoins.com wallet, you should still not consider them completely yours until you transfer them to your offline, secure Bitcoin wallet. Always remember to keep your private key private and share it with no one else.

If you already have an offline wallet, then transferring the fund there is easy, fast and secure. Simply copy the offline wallet's address onto the Wallet section of your www.localbitcoins.com. Once you do that, simply click the transfer button and the Bitcoins will be transferred to your offline Bitcoin wallet.

Confirm the transfer

Never conduct a transaction on your Bitcoin account without confirming it. Basically, every transaction ought to reflect on the Blockchain. Therefore, check and confirm the address where the Bitcoins were sent. This is often visible on the transaction ID. Now copy this ID down and save it somewhere.

Next, you need to get onto any website with Blockchain explorer. Once you find one, simply take the transaction ID and confirm whether it is authentic and if the Bitcoins actually are accredited to you. Block explorer allows users to check the status of any transaction just to confirm authenticity, origin and so on.

So when you check your wallet, you will gladly see the Bitcoins you just purchased. These Bitcoins do not exist in reality but only in digital form. They are in the form of a key, so to prove ownership you will need to show the key.

All Bitcoin users are aware of the fact that these Bitcoins are only in digital form. You will also need to your password when logging into your offline wallet and to your online Bitcoin account.

Always remember that the Bitcoin wallet is where your private key is stored. Most people assume this is where the Bitcoins are stored, but this is not accurate. As mentioned earlier, the Bitcoins you purchase come with two different keys. One is a public key, and the other is a private key.

The private key can compare to an ATM PIN or personal identity number. This key guards your Bitcoins and keeps them secure. Even when transactions occur, they can be viewed and confirmed. Therefore, this key should be kept as secure as possible and all transactions should be confirmed through the Blockchain.

The Bitcoins that you now own can be used to purchase goods, pay for services and even sent to people you want. To send or spend the Bitcoins, you will require the address of the recipient. This address is necessary for the transaction to be processed. The Blockchain can manage the transaction as required and will diligently transact on your behalf.

There are plenty of places where Bitcoin is accepted. There are businesses such as restaurants, hotels, gas stations, grocery stores and many others. A good number of small and large retailers accept Bitcoins, making it an important medium of transacting business.

Bitcoin is also accepted in other countries around the world. For instance, Japan, France, Canada, Australia and many others. While it is homogenous in nature, Bitcoin value varies in different countries due to the exchange rate. It also varies due to some of the premiums charged locally. When transacting internationally, it is important to take note of these charges and costs to avoid unnecessary losses.

Chapter 6: Trading in Bitcoins

One of the easiest and fastest ways of making money is trading in Bitcoins. The reason for this is due to the volatile nature of Bitcoins. It has recently been gaining in value at unprecedented rates.

Plenty of investors consider it a high risk, high reward type of investment. No one really has any idea how high its value will rise on any given day or how low. Fortunately, there are safe and profitable ways of trading in Bitcoins.

Trading in Bitcoins

Investors who trade in Bitcoin do so by trying to cash in on its global popularity. As demand for this cryptocurrency rises, so does its value. While the rewards can be very attractive, there is a certain level of risk, like with most investments, and this should be taken into account. Therefore, even as you trade in Bitcoins, make calculated risks and spend what you can afford to lose.

How Bitcoin trade works

Remember that Bitcoin is a form of currency just like any other. The only difference is that it is in digital form. Otherwise, it can be saved, invested and spent. You can also engage in trade using Bitcoins.

Remember also that Bitcoins are generated through mining. This is a complex process that is generated by solving algorithms using advanced hardware. After it has been decrypted, a single block can generate about 50 Bitcoins.

The time it takes to solve a mining algorithm depends mostly on the skill of the miner and the computer power they possess. However, this is mostly a lengthy and tedious process, so most investors prefer to trade in Bitcoins instead.

Trading in Bitcoins

Trade in Bitcoins operates just like it does in the stock market. And just like it is with securities, you buy at a low price and sell at a higher price. Therefore, you should consider the prospect of purchasing Bitcoins at a lower price and then sell them at a higher price.

The first step necessary is to create an account at any reputable online Bitcoin exchange. This is a process that has been discussed at length in previous chapters, so it is important to confirm the steps and then proceed. Once you have an account with an online Bitcoin exchange, open a personal wallet where you will keep your Bitcoin key.

The next step now is to monitor the Bitcoin market and watch the performance of this cryptocurrency. This you can still do at the same exchange where you purchased the Bitcoins. Examples of popular exchanges are BitStamp and Mt. Gox.

How the Bitcoin Exchange Works

At the Bitcoin exchange, you will be trading your Bitcoins for other currencies. Remember that Bitcoin is a currency, albeit, digital. There are many other currencies as well. They include the US dollar, EU euro, Japanese yen and so on. Each currency has a different value depending on a number of factors such as a country's wealth.

Bitcoin is traded on the exchange like a commodity similar to gold and oil. However, many of the exchanges that deal in Bitcoins usually trade Bitcoins to dollars and then to other currencies from other countries. They also receive currencies of different countries, convert these into dollars and then into Bitcoins.

Trading at the Bitcoin exchange directly

To make money, you need to time when the currencies have either gained or lost in value. Once you determine the appropriate moment, you may then go ahead and place your trades. This should lead you to make some profit. Now when the value of Bitcoin falls significantly, it will be time to buy and then hold, until it rises before selling again.

Trading through a Bitcoin broker

Apart from trading at the Bitcoin by yourself, you may also trade via a registered Bitcoin broker. This is an expert broker who can successfully place trades and make money on your behalf. The broker will also monitor the market for you and also keep your earnings safely.

Pointers to keep in mind

- The first step in trading with Bitcoins is to select an exchange and then open an account

- Once the account is up and running, proceed to purchase Bitcoins from the exchange and then transfer the Bitcoins to your wallet

- Now identify some other exchanges and start monitoring the performance of Bitcoin. You will be looking out for fluctuation in its value or price.

- Identify a strategy that favors you and one that will ensure you maximize profitability while minimizing losses

It is important to keep in mind that, although Bitcoin trading is easy, you need to be aware of the potential risk of any kind of investment. As usual, there are risks of losing your money, so take precautions as necessary.

Remember that is very important to safely and securely store your Bitcoins. An offline secure wallet is a much better option where you are fully in charge. Follow the steps described in previous chapters to ensure you open an offline wallet and secure your Bitcoins here. If you store your Bitcoins online, ensure that your computer has the necessary protections against hacking and viruses. Also store your Bitcoins online with a reputable and trustworthy firm.

Understanding how Bitcoin exchanges work

Bitcoins exchanges work in a similar manner to physical currency exchanges. This means that you are simply using one currency to purchase another. The only difference is that Bitcoin is not a physical currency but a cryptocurrency.

Mining the Bitcoin

Some claim this is the easiest but slowest means of generating Bitcoins. All you need to do is dedicate one computer to solving or decrypting blocks that then produce the Bitcoins. You will need a powerful computer running the latest Bitcoin-mining software.

The regular PC will take you a little over a year to complete deciphering on Bitcoin block. This is considered rather costly and not worth the time or effort. If you choose to go down this path, consider going for a better computer, but it will cost you.

One of the best in the market today is the 128 GHS Bitcoin Miner. This computer costs about $2,400 and was developed by the firm known as Advance Mining Technology. Lately, however, the cost of mining Bitcoins has become so expensive that it is hardly worth anyone's time.

Gang up with other miners

Rather than engaging in a Bitcoin mining operation on your own as an individual, you may choose to join other miners and pool your resources together. Such grouping for purposes of mining Bitcoins is known as a mining pool.

The puzzle to be deciphered can be broken up into pieces and solved by every member of the team using their powerful computers. As soon as the deciphering process is complete, members get paid for the part they contributed in deciphering the block.

There is a certain level of scrutiny among participants in the mining pool. They are required to provide some form of authentication such as a BTC username or a 2-step Google authentication code. Fortunately, Bitcoin is still pretty anonymous, and so no personal details of any of the pool members will be required. This is great because this is information that cannot be compromised. However, in all cases, take precautions because money and strangers provide some concerns.

Trading Bitcoins at the markets

Trading in Bitcoins at the market is considered the best, fastest method of earning profits. However, it is also the riskiest. Regardless of the cryptocurrency exchange that you choose, you will have to create an account which means verifying your identity using a proof of address document and a government-issued identity card. However, if you already have some type of cryptocurrency in hand when you come to a new exchange then you can likely get started without any type of verification required.

Once this process is complete, then all you will need to do is to deposit funds into your account and start watching the market. The best approach is to watch the market for a couple of days, like at daily, weekly and monthly trades and then finally proceed to initiate your trade and make some money.

Each exchange charges a transaction fee on top of what the Bitcoin blockchain charges per transaction. These fees are going to vary per exchange and will either be a set rate, or a variable percentage of the total amount traded. If you are planning to make lots of small trades then you are going to want to go with an exchange that charges a percentage of each transaction while if you are going to be making a few larger trades you will want to choose an exchange with a set rate. Just like with all other trades, Bitcoin trade can be very risky. If you do not properly understand the trading market, you may incur some losses, so please be very cautious.

Rewards and risks of trading in Bitcoins

It is important to note that the value of Bitcoin varies dramatically at any point during the trading period. Regular currencies from major trading nations such as those from Western Europe and North America do not fluctuate dramatically but within a reasonable range.

On the contrary, Bitcoins value varies greatly, so the chances of making a good profit are great. But then so are the risks of incurring a loss. In fact, Bitcoin losses would be significantly larger than those incurred on forex trade for a similar dollar amount. This is because of the way Bitcoin is denominated as well as its volatility.

To avoid arbitrage, most traders offload their Bitcoins as soon as they can. This is also one of the major causes of volatility of the Bitcoin. If investors were to hold onto their Bitcoins a little longer, it would become more stable and less volatile.

Profitability is also possible with a super-long view of the market. For instance, investors who bought Bitcoins at less than $100 back in 2012 made over 600% in returns on their investments. While the sub $100 prices are not likely to come back any soon, long term investment in Bitcoins is not a bad idea at all.

Is Bitcoin subject to taxation?

According to financial writers, Bitcoin is considered taxable anytime a taxable event occurs. For instance, if Bitcoins are converted into dollars or other tangible currency as a profit, then this profit will be subject to taxation. The same applies when you trade Bitcoins for a product or service.

When it comes to taxation, Bitcoin is considered an asset and not a currency. Just the same way gold is considered. If it is sold for a profit, then the profit is subject to taxation. Similarly, if it is traded in an exchange and a profit is realized, then this profit is subject to taxation.

Safety of Your Bitcoins

You may want to consider your Bitcoin wallet the same way you would a real wallet full of cash. First, you should not store all your Bitcoins in a single wallet. You will be much safer if you distribute the Bitcoins to a number of digital wallets.

Since there is no foolproof method of securing your Bitcoin wallet, the best security measures to take is to back up your wallet and encrypt it. You should then make several copies of the wallet and then distribute them across several secure servers.

The Bitcoin has enjoyed meteoric rise over the last couple of years. This reason, together with the relatively low risk of getting caught, has made it a prime target for hackers and cyber criminals.

Be cautious

Plenty of people and organizations have lost Bitcoins in one way or other. Some of the major losses have been occasioned by hackers while others were due to technical problems.

Take for instance the firm Bitomat.pl. This is a Bitcoin mining company that lost 17000 Bitcoins after a routine maintenance on their main servers went horribly wrong. The Bitcoins were worth more than $14 million. Apparently, the server hosting the firm's digital wallet ate itself completely.

A trading place known as The Sheep Marketplace had over 96,000 BTC stolen after their systems were hacked. Their loss was to the tune of $220 million. Cyber criminals and hackers use all sorts of tricks to steal Bitcoins. Their methods include phishing, social engineering, use of malicious software or malware and all other tricks. Caution is therefore very important when trading Bitcoins.

How to start accepting and using Bitcoins for businesses

Many businesses today have started accepting payments in Bitcoins. There is a good reason for this. More and more people are transacting in Bitcoins and using them as a preferred digital currency.

Today, anyone operating a legitimate business selling goods or providing services can easily start accepting Bitcoins as a form of payment. Such businesses may be looking for an additional form of payment, especially for online transactions.

Many business owners have been wondering about the best way to accommodate the use of Bitcoins for their businesses. This is because Bitcoins have been touted as offering an alternative to cash and enabling users to evade taxes and so on.

Business owners are wary of conflicting with laws and government, so they want to ensure that they pay taxes as required even on income generated through trade using Bitcoins.

Where to start

Start with a sign
It is important to get the "Bitcoin Accepted Here" sign. This lets your customers know that your business is Bitcoin friendly and that they can use their Bitcoins to pay for goods and services that you offer.

You will also need to let your customers know that they should contact the business if they are to pay with Bitcoins. Even customers who do not use Bitcoins will be happy to know that now they have an additional form of payment that they can use.

Accepting Bitcoins for payment

You can accept Bitcoins whether you are a brick and mortar establishment or an online business. For brick and mortar establishments such as stores and restaurants, then you will need to install hardware terminals and apps.

You could also provide a simple wallet address which makes use of QR codes. When it comes to online stores and shops, then it is best to get a good programmer to prepare the Bitcoins payment platform complete with a full node.

Accepting payments through a Smartphone or Tablet. You also have the option, as a business, to start using a web app or a dedicated application program. There are plenty of wallets that now accept Bitcoins and support use of QR code scanning.

Accounting for Bitcoin payments

You may need to keep tabs of all Bitcoin payments for accounting purposes. You should then issue receipts to your customers and also keep a record of the transaction for accounting purposes.

Have your customers sign an agreement or contract

Having a contract with your customers is important so that there is no disagreement or misunderstanding later on. For instance, you may wish to let your customers know that they are responsible for paying transactional costs when using Bitcoin payments. The contract should also include things such as the use of escrow service, dispute resolution, and refund policy.

Tax compliance with Bitcoin payments

Even as you receive Bitcoin payments at your business, you should consider making arrangements to pay taxes accruing from your Bitcoins transactions. There is plenty of debate and lack of clarity on how to treat such transactions. This is caused by a lack of guidance from the IRS and differences in exchange rates and transaction fees.

The general rule, therefore, is to note any income resulting from Bitcoin payments and also noting any costs incurred as a result of Bitcoin processing. These should both be reported and then the income, and subsequently, tax due calculated.

Important factors when using Bitcoin for business

You get to choose your own fees
Traders and business owners are not charged any fees to receive Bitcoins. A lot of Bitcoin wallets

allow you to set your own transaction fees. The wallets also charge reasonable fees. Higher fees will always discourage customers who may then prefer alternative payment solutions.

Guard against fraudulent activity

You need to protect your customers and business against any chance of fraud. With other platforms such as PayPal and credit cards, there are measures in place that guard against fraudulent activity. Since Bitcoin payment and charges cannot be reversed, you should take extra caution to prevent fraud.

International payments are very fast

One of the benefits of using Bitcoins is that payments are processed very fast. It takes the same time to send a payment across the street as it is to an international destination. Banks often make you wait up to 3 or more days to process international payments. Such delays are absent when receiving Bitcoins.

Let people know you use Bitcoins

There are more and more people in the US and around the world who are now using Bitcoins. All these people want to find stores and outlets that accept them. By advertising and getting the word out there, your customers and the general public will gladly trade with you. Customers also love choice when it comes to payment systems.

Use multi-signature for added protection

It is a good thing that Bitcoin uses multi-signature feature for added protection. This allows payment to be made after approval by more than one person. This ensures that only authorized spending is allowed.

In many countries, Bitcoin has been recognized formally by finance regulators and governments as a form of currency. In practice, however, Bitcoin payments are similar to payments made with credit cards, PayPal, and other payment systems.

Plenty of people love the anonymous nature of Bitcoins because it does not leave a paper trail. All transactions are anonymous and cannot be reversed. However, in business, Bitcoin payments are considered simply as an alternative for those who prefer to pay in this cryptocurrency.

Bitcoin Payments from Wallet to Checkout

As a trader, you can now find ready-made Bitcoin solutions suitable for your business. Most of these solutions can be customized to fit specific needs that individual businesses may have.

Solutions that are currently available from firms like www.bitpay.com allow businesses to accept retail Bitcoin payments complete with donation tools and billing. The funds, once received, can be deposit as cash in dollar amounts to the bank.

This payment solution has been designed to minimize fraud risks and to instantly convert Bitcoins into other currencies that can then be transacted as desired. Customers who sign up will receive a Bitcoin wallet which they can then use to receive, store and send Bitcoins. A secure, open source app can provide the payment solution that your business needs.

Get the bitpay Visa Card

The site bitcoin.com offers a Visa card that enables users, such as traders to receive Bitcoins and then convert these to dollars which they can then spend freely. The dollars can be loaded onto the bitpay card seamlessly, making the process a safe, fast and convenient option for traders.

Choosing the Right Bitcoin Wallet

A good, secure and safe wallet is what you need if you are to keep your Bitcoins secure. Finding the right one can be tricky, but the important considerations should be privacy, long term storage, and simplicity.

First, it is advisable to have more than one single wallet. This way, you minimize the risk of losing all your Bitcoins and also introduce different wallets for different applications.

Bitcoin banks offer their customers a choice of wallets. However, these are considered temporary solutions that are best used when buying, selling or spending Bitcoins. They should not be considered long term solutions.

There are high privacy wallets available for those who need very high privacy. They add extra layers of protection to hide the user's activity and make it harder for hackers to penetrate.

Hardware wallets are considered as important wallets offering useful and above-average security solution. With this kind of solution, Bitcoins are stored offline but can be spent from anywhere.

Hackers can definitely not get anywhere close to these wallets.

Also available for long term storage are paper wallets. With this solution, you write down the key on a piece of paper. This is often done by a printer that prints out the Bitcoin address. You will need to trust the software or code that generates the wallet.

However, remember that even with paper wallets, you will still need a digital wallet when it comes to spending the Bitcoins or cashing in. therefore, paper wallets are mostly considered for long term purposes.

Ensure that you use a very strong password with your Bitcoin wallet. A strong password should have about 20 alphanumeric characters. It should have both uppercase and lowercase letters as well as nonalphabet characters such as the dollar sign, pound sign or exclamation mark.

Conclusion

Thanks for making it through to the end of this book, let's hope it was informative and able to provide you with all of the tools you need to achieve your goals whatever they may be.

The next step is to take your time and read this information carefully. It will help you understand all there is to know about Bitcoins, how they are mined, their volatile nature and how you can spend them or send to friends and family.

Bitcoins are very popular as a means of generating wealth. Plenty of people have made good returns after investing their money in Bitcoin. Its value has continued to rise at a phenomenal rate over the years. If you read the chapter on investing in Bitcoin, then you may learn more about how to invest your money in this cryptocurrency and how to earn long term, attractive returns.

This book is by no means exhaustive on all things about Bitcoin. While the information provided here is useful, there is plenty more available online. So, get informed to enable you to make wise decisions in the future. If you choose to invest in Bitcoins, you should then find out everything you need to know about Bitcoin investing.

Always remember that security is key if you are to trade or deal in Bitcoins. This online currency has a very anonymous nature, and transactions cannot be reversed. There is very little threat of getting caught, so hackers and scammers are emboldened by this fact. Ensure that your website is protected by multiple layers of firewalls and antivirus programs. Always opt for encrypted solutions for transactions to maintain their integrity and reduce chances of compromise.

Bitcoin is a very volatile online currency and chances of losing money are high if you have very little skill and knowledge on investing. Therefore, first learn all there is to know about trading and then understand how to trade in such a volatile currency.

Finally, if you found this book useful in any way, a review on Amazon is always appreciated!

www.ingramcontent.com/pod-product-compliance
Lightning Source LLC
Chambersburg PA
CBHW070311230526
45470CB00002B/822